Valentine Delights
A Daily Journal

Hood Holiday Journal Series – Book 2

Karen Jean Matsko Hood

Valentine Delights
A Daily Journal
Hood Holiday Journal Series – Book 2

Gift Inscription

To: _____

From: _____

Date: _____

Special Message: _____

_____

_____

_____

_____

_____

It is always nice to receive a personal note to
create a special memory.

www.ValentineDelights.com
www.WhisperingPinePress.com
www.WhisperingPinePressBookstore.com

Valentine Delights
A Daily Journal

Hood Holiday Journal Series – Book 2

Karen Jean Matsko Hood

Published by:

Whispering Pine Press International, Inc.
Your Northwest Book Publishing Company

P.O. Box 214
Spokane Valley, WA 99037-0214 USA
Phone: (509) 928-8700 | Fax: (509) 922-9949
Websites: www.WhisperingPinePress.com
www.WhisperingPinePressBookstore.com
Blog: www.WhisperingPinePressBlog.com
Email: sales@WhisperingPinePress.com
SAN 253-200X
Printed in the U.S.A.

Published by Whispering Pine Press International, Inc.
P.O. Box 214
Spokane Valley, Washington 99037-0214 USA

For sales outside the United States, please contact the Whispering Pine Press International, Inc., International Sales Department.

Manufactured in the United States of America. This paper is acid-free and 100% chlorine free.

Book and Cover Design by Artistic Design Service, Inc.
P.O. Box 1782
Spokane Valley, WA 99037-1782 USA
www.ArtisticDesignService.com

Library of Congress Number LCCN: 2014900296

Hood, Karen Jean Matsko
    Title: Valentine Delights: A Daily Journal, Hood Holiday Journal Series –
Book 2

    p.   cm.

ISBN: 978-1-59210-093-4   case bound
ISBN: 978-1-59210-094-1   perfect bound
ISBN: 978-1-59649-296-7   E-PDF
ISBN: 978-1-59210-095-8   E-PUB
ISBN: 978-1-59434-817-4   E-PRC

First Edition: January 2014
1. Journal (*Valentine Delights: A Daily Journal, Hood Holiday Journal Series – Book 2*)
1. Title

Valentine Delights
A Daily Journal
Hood Holiday Journal Series – Book 2

Table of Contents

Colors and Symbolism of Flowers and Herbs

(In Alphabetical order)

It is interesting to know the symbolism behind the flowers you select for Valentine messages.

Acacia

elegance, friendship, secret love, chaste love, beauty in retirement

Allspice

compassion

Almond

hope, lovers' charm

Aloe

grief

_____

_____

_____

_____

_____

_____

_____

_____

_____

_____

_____

_____

_____

_____

_____

_____

_____

_____

_____

_____

_____

_____

_____

_____

_____

Amaranth

fidelity

_____
_____
_____
_____
_____
_____
_____
_____
_____
_____
_____
_____
_____
_____
_____
_____
_____
_____
_____
_____
_____
_____
_____
_____
_____
_____

Amaryllis

splendid beauty; pride, timidity

February 15th was the date of the Roman festival of Lupercalia - where young men held a lottery to decide which girl would be theirs.

Ambrosia

returned love

_____
_____
_____
_____
_____
_____
_____
_____
_____
_____
_____
_____
_____
_____
_____
_____
_____
_____
_____
_____
_____
_____
_____
_____
_____
_____

Amethyst

admiration, undying love

_____
_____
_____
_____
_____
_____
_____
_____
_____
_____
_____
_____
_____
_____
_____
_____
_____
_____
_____
_____
_____
_____
_____
_____
_____
_____
_____
_____

Anemone

truth, unfading love, sincerity, anticipation, forsaken, fading hope

Angelica

inspiration

Aniseed

restoration of youth

_____

_____

_____

_____

_____

_____

_____

_____

_____

_____

_____

_____

_____

_____

_____

_____

_____

_____

_____

_____

_____

_____

_____

_____

_____

Apple (Blossom)

preference, good fortune

The Taj Mahal at Agra, India is perhaps the most splendid gift of love. It was built by the Mughal Emperor Shah Jahan in memory of his beautiful wife, Mumtaz Mahal. Work on the Taj began in 1634 and continued for almost 22 years. It took the labor of 20,000 workers from all over India and Central Asia.

Arum

ardor

Azalea

temperance, fragile passion, Chinese symbol of womanhood, take care of yourself

Baby's Breath

everlasting love, pure in heart, happiness

Basil (Sweet)

best wishes, love, hatred

_____
_____
_____
_____
_____
_____
_____
_____
_____
_____
_____
_____
_____
_____
_____
_____
_____
_____
_____
_____
_____
_____
_____
_____
_____
_____

Bachelor's Buttons

single blessedness, hope in love, celibacy

_____
_____
_____
_____
_____
_____
_____
_____
_____
_____
_____
_____
_____
_____
_____
_____
_____
_____
_____
_____
_____
_____
_____
_____
_____
_____
_____
_____

Bells of Ireland

good luck

_____

_____

_____

_____

_____

_____

_____

_____

_____

_____

_____

_____

_____

_____

_____

_____

_____

_____

_____

_____

During the late 1800s, postage rates around the world dropped, and the obscene St. Valentine's Day card became popular, despite the Victorian era being otherwise very prudish. As the numbers of racy valentines grew, several countries banned the practice of exchanging Valentine's Days cards. During this period, Chicago's post office rejected more than 25,000 cards on the grounds that they were so indecent, they were not fit to be carried through the U.S. mail.

Bluebell

humility, constancy

Buttercup

childishness, ingratitude

Broom

humility, neatness

Cactus

warmth, endurance, grandeur

Calla

magnificent beauty

Camellia

you're adorable, longing, a flame in my heart

February 14, 270 A.D. : Roman Emperor Claudius II, dubbed "Claudius the Cruel," beheaded a priest named Valentine for performing marriage ceremonies. Claudius II had outlawed marriages when Roman men began refusing to go to war in order to stay with their wives.

Cedar

I live for thee, think of me

Chamomile

patience, attracts wealth

Chickweed

meet me, rendezvous

_____
_____
_____
_____
_____
_____
_____
_____
_____
_____
_____
_____
_____
_____
_____
_____
_____
_____
_____
_____
_____
_____
_____
_____
_____
_____
_____
_____

Chrysanthemum, red

love you

Chrysanthemum, white

truth

_____
_____
_____
_____
_____
_____
_____
_____
_____
_____
_____
_____
_____
_____
_____
_____
_____
_____
_____
_____
_____
_____
_____
_____
_____
_____
_____
_____

Chrysanthemum, yellow

slighted

Clover Four Leaved

good luck, be mine

_____
_____
_____
_____
_____
_____
_____
_____
_____
_____
_____
_____
_____
_____
_____
_____
_____
_____
_____
_____
_____
_____
_____
_____
_____

Coriander

lust

_____
_____
_____
_____
_____
_____
_____
_____
_____
_____
_____
_____
_____
_____
_____
_____
_____
_____
_____
_____
_____
_____
_____
_____
_____
_____
_____

Cowslip

pensiveness, winning grace

Crocus

cheerfulness, abuse not, joy

Daisy

innocence, purity, faith, simplicity

Daffodil

regards, deceit, unrequited love

In Wales, wooden love spoons were carved and given as gifts on February 14th. Hearts, keys and keyholes were favorite decorations on the spoons. The decoration meant, "You unlock my heart!"

Dandelion

wishes come true, faithfulness, rustic oracle

Dogwood

durability

_____
_____
_____
_____
_____
_____
_____
_____
_____
_____
_____
_____
_____
_____
_____
_____
_____
_____
_____
_____
_____
_____
_____
_____
_____
_____
_____
_____
_____

Elm

dignity

_____
_____
_____
_____
_____
_____
_____
_____
_____
_____
_____
_____
_____
_____
_____
_____
_____
_____
_____
_____
_____
_____
_____
_____
_____
_____
_____
_____
_____
_____

Eucalyptus

protection

Fennel

worthy of all praise, strength

_____
_____
_____
_____
_____
_____
_____
_____
_____
_____
_____
_____
_____
_____
_____
_____
_____
_____
_____
_____
_____
_____
_____
_____
_____
_____
_____
_____

Fern

sincerity, confidence and shelter

_____

_____

_____

_____

_____

_____

_____

_____

_____

_____

_____

_____

_____

_____

_____

_____

_____

_____

_____

_____

_____

_____

One single perfect red rose framed with baby's breath is referred to by
some florists as a "signature rose," and is the preferred choice for many for
giving on Valentine's Day, anniversary, or birthday.

Forget Me Not

don't forget me, true love, memories

_____
_____
_____
_____
_____
_____
_____
_____
_____
_____
_____
_____
_____
_____
_____
_____
_____
_____
_____
_____
_____
_____
_____
_____
_____

Garlic

courage, strength

Geranium

friendship, preference

Gladiolus

love at first sight, strength of character

Grass

submission, utility

_____
_____
_____
_____
_____
_____
_____
_____
_____
_____
_____
_____
_____
_____
_____
_____
_____
_____
_____
_____
_____
_____
_____
_____
_____
_____
_____
_____
_____

Hazelnut

reconciliation

Heliotrope

devotion, eternal love, faithfulness

Hibiscus

delicate beauty

Hollyhock

female ambition

_____
_____
_____
_____
_____
_____
_____
_____
_____
_____
_____
_____
_____
_____
_____
_____
_____
_____
_____
_____
_____
_____
_____
_____
_____
_____

Honesty

honesty, fascination

___

Some people used to believe that if a woman saw a robin flying overhead on Valentine's Day, it meant she would marry a sailor. If she saw a sparrow, she would marry a poor man and be very happy. If she saw a goldfinch, she would marry a millionaire.

Honeysuckle

generous and devoted affection, sweetness of disposition

Iris

faith, hope, wisdom and valor, eloquence, message

Ivy

fidelity, friendship, affection, marriage

Jasmine

cheerful, wealth, gracefulness

_____

_____

_____

_____

_____

_____

_____

_____

_____

_____

_____

_____

_____

_____

_____

_____

_____

_____

_____

_____

_____

_____

_____

_____

_____

_____

_____

_____

Jonquil

desire, return my affection, sympathy

Juniper
protection

The ancient Romans celebrated the Feast of Lupercalia in honor of Juno, the queen of the Roman gods and goddesses on February 14. Juno was also the goddess of women and marriage.

Lavender

devotion, distrust

Laurel

glory, ambition

Lemon

zest, brings love

_____
_____
_____
_____
_____
_____
_____
_____
_____
_____
_____
_____
_____
_____
_____
_____
_____
_____
_____
_____
_____
_____
_____
_____
_____

Lilac

first love

_____
_____
_____
_____
_____
_____
_____
_____
_____
_____
_____
_____
_____
_____
_____
_____
_____
_____
_____
_____
_____
_____
_____
_____
_____
_____
_____
_____
_____
_____

Lily

heavenly, purity of heart

Lime Tree

conjugal love

_____
_____
_____
_____
_____
_____
_____
_____
_____
_____
_____
_____
_____
_____
_____
_____
_____
_____
_____
_____
_____
_____
_____
_____
_____

The first photograph of a U.S. President was taken on February 14, 1849 by Matthew Brady in New York City. President James Polk was the subject of the famous picture. .

Liverwort

confidence

_____
_____
_____
_____
_____
_____
_____
_____
_____
_____
_____
_____
_____
_____
_____
_____
_____
_____
_____
_____
_____
_____
_____
_____
_____
_____
_____
_____

Lobelia

malevolence

_____
_____
_____
_____
_____
_____
_____
_____
_____
_____
_____
_____
_____
_____
_____
_____
_____
_____
_____
_____
_____
_____
_____
_____
_____
_____

Lily of the Valley

return to happiness

Marigold

comfort the heart, grief, jealousy

Marjoram

blushes, joy and happiness

Mimosa

sensitivity

Mistletoe

kiss me, I surmount difficulties

_____
_____
_____
_____
_____
_____
_____
_____
_____
_____
_____
_____
_____
_____
_____
_____
_____
_____
_____
_____
_____
_____
_____
_____
_____
_____

Myrtle

love, love in absence, remembrance

_____

_____

_____

_____

_____

_____

_____

_____

_____

_____

_____

_____

_____

_____

_____

_____

_____

_____

_____

_____

_____

_____

_____

_____

The Italian city of Verona, where Shakespeare's lovers Romeo and Juliet lived, receives about 1,000 letters addressed to Juliet every Valentine's Day.

Narcissus

formality, stay sweet

Olive

peace

_____
_____
_____
_____
_____
_____
_____
_____
_____
_____
_____
_____
_____
_____
_____
_____
_____
_____
_____
_____
_____
_____
_____
_____
_____
_____
_____
_____
_____
_____

Oleander

caution, beware

Orchid

love, beauty, flattery

_____
_____
_____
_____
_____
_____
_____
_____
_____
_____
_____
_____
_____
_____
_____
_____
_____
_____
_____
_____
_____
_____
_____
_____
_____
_____
_____

Pansy

thoughts for you, love

Peach Blossom

I am yours, captive

_____

_____

_____

_____

_____

_____

_____

_____

_____

_____

_____

_____

_____

_____

_____

_____

_____

_____

_____

_____

_____

_____

_____

_____

The Kama Sutra is believed to be the oldest sex manual in existence. Generally considered the standard work on love in Sanskrit literature, the book is thought to have been written around 300 A.D.

Peony

shame, bashfulness, indignation, anger

_____
_____
_____
_____
_____
_____
_____
_____
_____
_____
_____
_____
_____
_____
_____
_____
_____
_____
_____
_____
_____
_____
_____

Periwinkle, Blue

early friendship

_____
_____
_____
_____
_____
_____
_____
_____
_____
_____
_____
_____
_____
_____
_____
_____
_____
_____
_____
_____
_____
_____
_____
_____
_____
_____

Periwinkle, White

pleasures of memory

_____
_____
_____
_____
_____
_____
_____
_____
_____
_____
_____
_____
_____
_____
_____
_____
_____
_____
_____
_____
_____
_____
_____
_____

Peruvian Heliotrope

devoted to you

_____
_____
_____
_____
_____
_____
_____
_____
_____
_____
_____
_____
_____
_____
_____
_____
_____
_____
_____
_____
_____
_____
_____
_____
_____

The oldest known Valentines were sent in 1415 A.D. by the Duke of Orleans to his French wife while he was imprisoned in the Tower of London. It is still on display in a museum in England.

Petunia

never despair, anger, resentment

Poinsettia

of good cheer

_____

_____

_____

_____

_____

_____

_____

_____

_____

_____

_____

_____

_____

_____

_____

_____

_____

_____

_____

_____

_____

_____

_____

_____

_____

Poppy

eternal sleep, oblivion, imagination, extravagance

Prickly Pear

satire

_____
_____
_____
_____
_____
_____
_____
_____
_____
_____
_____
_____
_____
_____
_____
_____
_____
_____
_____
_____
_____
_____
_____
_____
_____
_____

Primrose

can't live without you, early youth, young love

Plum Tree

fidelity, promises

_____
_____
_____
_____
_____
_____
_____
_____
_____
_____
_____
_____
_____
_____
_____
_____
_____
_____
_____
_____
_____
_____
_____
_____
_____

The red rose was the favorite flower of Venus, the Roman goddess of love.
Red stands for strong feelings which is why a red rose is a flower of love.

Roses

love, innocence, heavenly, secrecy and silence, happiness, believe me, jealousy, unity, love at first sight, still love you

Rosebuds

youth, a heart innocent of love, pure and lovely, girlhood

_____
_____
_____
_____
_____
_____
_____
_____
_____
_____
_____
_____
_____
_____
_____
_____
_____
_____
_____
_____
_____
_____
_____
_____
_____
_____

Rose leaf

you may hope

_____
_____
_____
_____
_____
_____
_____
_____
_____
_____
_____
_____
_____
_____
_____
_____
_____
_____
_____
_____
_____
_____
_____
_____
_____
_____

Rosemary

remembrance, commitment, fidelity

Sage

wisdom, long life, domestic virtue

Shamrock

lightheartedness

_____

Wearing a wedding ring on the fourth finger of the left hand dates back to ancient Egypt, where it was believed that the vein of love ran from this finger directly to the heart.

Snapdragon

no, deception, gracious lady, presumption

Snowdrop

hope

Sorrel

with affection

_____
_____
_____
_____
_____
_____
_____
_____
_____
_____
_____
_____
_____
_____
_____
_____
_____
_____
_____
_____
_____
_____
_____
_____

Spanish Jasmine

sexy, sensual

Chocolate manufacturers currently use 40 percent of the world's almonds and 20 percent of the world's peanuts.

Spearmint

warm feelings

Spider flower

elope with me

_____

_____

_____

_____

_____

_____

_____

_____

_____

_____

_____

_____

_____

_____

_____

_____

_____

_____

_____

_____

_____

_____

_____

_____

_____

_____

_____

_____

Sweet pea

goodbye, blissful pleasure, thank you for a lovely time

_____
_____
_____
_____
_____
_____
_____
_____
_____
_____
_____
_____
_____
_____
_____
_____
_____
_____
_____
_____
_____
_____
_____
_____
_____
_____
_____
_____

Thyme

strength and courage

Tuberose

dangerous pleasure

Tulip

fame, charity, love, beautiful eyes, hopeless love, believe me

_____

_____

_____

_____

_____

_____

_____

_____

_____

_____

_____

_____

_____

_____

_____

_____

_____

_____

_____

_____

_____

_____

_____

_____

_____

_____

_____

February 22, 1998, Tori Amos, singer & Mark Hawley, British sound engineer. She wore a floor-length silver cape over her ice-blue gown. February 24, 1992 Kurt Cobain & Diva Courtney Love

Valerian

an accommodating disposition

Veronica

fidelity

_____
_____
_____
_____
_____
_____
_____
_____
_____
_____
_____
_____
_____
_____
_____
_____
_____
_____
_____
_____
_____
_____
_____
_____
_____
_____

Violet

modesty, faithfulness\

Wallflower

fidelity in adversity

_____
_____
_____
_____
_____
_____
_____
_____
_____
_____
_____
_____
_____
_____
_____
_____
_____
_____
_____
_____
_____
_____
_____
_____

February 22, 1998, Tori Amos, singer & Mark Hawley, British sound engineer. She wore a floor-length silver cape over her ice-blue gown. February 24, 1992 Kurt Cobain & Diva Courtney Love

Dedications

To my husband and best friend, Jim.

To our seventeen children: Gabriel, Brianne Kristina and her husband Moulik Vinodkumar Kothari, Marissa Kimberly and her husband Kevin Matthew Franck, Janelle Karina and her husband Paul Joseph Turcotte, Mikayla Karlene, Kyler James, Kelsey Katrina, Corbin Joel, Caleb Jerome, Keisha Kalani Hiwot, Devontay Joshua, Kianna Karielle Selam, Rosy Kiara, Mercedes Katherine, Jasmine Khalia Wengel, Cheyenne Krystal, and Annalise Kaylee Marie.

To our grandchildren and foster grandchildren: Courtney, Lorenzo, and Leah.

To my brother, Stephen, and his wife, Karen.

To my husband's ten siblings: Gary, Colleen, John, Dan, Mary, Ray, Ann, Teresa, Barbara, Agnes, and their families.

In loving memory of my mom, who passed away in 2007; my dad, who passed away in 1976; and my sister, Sandy, who passed away due to multiple sclerosis in 1999.

To Sandy's three sons: Monte, Bradley, and Derek. To Monte's wife, Sarah, and their children: Liam, Alice, Charlie, Samuel and their foster children. To Bradley's wife, Shawnda, and their children: Anton, Isaac, and Isabel.

To our foster children past and present: Krystal, Sara, Rebecca, Janice, Devontay Joshua, Mercedes Katherine, Zha'Nell, Makia, Onna, Cheyenne Krystal, Onna Marie, Nevaeh, and Zada, our future foster children, and all foster children everywhere.

To the Court Appointed Special Advocate (CASA) Volunteer Program in the judicial system which benefits abused and neglected children.

To the Literacy Campaign dedicated to promoting literacy throughout the world.

Acknowledgements

The author would like to acknowledge all those individuals who helped me during my time in writing this book. Appreciation is extended for all their support and effort they put into this project.

Deep gratitude and profound thanks are owed to my husband, Jim, for giving freely of his time and encouragement during this project. Also, thanks are owed to my children Gabriel, Brianne Kristina and her husband Moulik Vinodkumar Kothari, Marissa Kimberly and her husband Kevin Matthew Franck, Janelle Karina and her husband Paul Joseph Turcotte, Mikayla Karlene, Kyler James, Kelsey Katrina, Corbin Joel, Caleb Jerome, Keisha Kalani Hiwot, Devontay Joshua, Kianna Karielle Selam, Rosy Kiara, Mercedes Katherine, Jasmine Khalia Wengel, Cheyenne Krystal, and Annalise Kaylee Marie. All of these persons inspire my writing.

Thanks are due to Sharron Thompson for her assistance in editing and typing this manuscript for publication. Thanks go to Artistic Design Service, Inc. for their assistance in formatting and providing a graphic design of this manuscript for publication. This project could not have been completed without them.

Many thanks are due to members of my family, all of whom were very supportive during the time it took to complete this project. Their patience and support are greatly appreciated.

Praise for Valentine Delights
A Daily Journal
Hood Holiday Journal Series – Book 2

…"Each year I like to search for fun, new, and creative ways to surprise my family on Valentines Day. Since discovering *Valentine Delights Journal*, I've been able to record my memories.

There are many ideas in this journal to help you show your children and friends just how much they mean to you. Treat yourself or someone you love to a copy of this journal today!"…

Kimberly Carter
Assistant

…"*Valentine Delights Journal* with its tidbits of romantic poetry, folklore, history, and other wonderful information is a must-have holiday book for any valentine lover.

Before buying any flowers, look in *Valentine Delights Journal* for information on the "Colors and Symbolism of Flowers" to find just the right flower to say the message you want to convey. This journal has short bits of information along with blank pages for you to write your own notes or recipes.

Valentine Delights Journal will soon be part of your treasured collection of splendid holiday records to be passed down to future generations."…

Mary Scripture-Smith
Graphic Designer

Praise for Valentine Delights

A Daily Journal
Hood Holiday Journal Series – Book 2

…"Whispering Pine Press International has done it again with the newest in their Cookbook Delights Holiday Series collection. *Valentine Delights Journal* continues the legacy of high quality work and craftsmanship from its author. The journal pages are designed to leave space to write your own journal notes and favorite recipes."…

Allyson Schnabel
Editor, Teacher

… "With the world as it is today it's easy to be distracted. We often put the ones we love most on the back burner. That's why Valentine's Day is so important. It gives us the chance to truly show how much we love that special someone.

Valentine Delights Journal is a companion to Valentine Delights Cookbook. It gives you space to write your own journal notes or your favorite recipes.

Valentine Delights Journal not only has tidbits of information, but it includes a full guide that explains the meaning behind a large array of plants and flowers. With this you can build a luscious bouquet that has its own unique story.

Sit down and enjoy this book. Share the poetry. Savor its delights, and cherish each other."…

Ed Archambeault
Spokane, WA.

Reader Feedback Form

Dear Reader,

    We are very interested in what our readers think. Please fill in the form below and return to:

Whispering Pine Press International, Inc.
c/o Valentine Delights: A Daily Journal
P.O. Box 214, Spokane Valley, WA 99037-0214
Phone: (509) 928-8700 | Fax: (509) 922-9949
Email: sales@WhisperingPinePress.com
Publisher Websites: www.WhisperingPinePress.com
www.WhisperingPinePressBookstore.com
Blog: www.WhisperingPinePressBlog.com

Name: _____

Address: _____

City, St., Zip: _____

Phone/Fax: (____) _____ | (____) _____

Email: _____

Comments/Suggestions: _____

_____

_____

_____

_____

    A great deal of care and attention has been exercised in the creation of this book. Designing a great cookbook that is original, fun, and easy to use has been a job that required many hours of diligence, creativity, and research. Although we strive to make this book completely error free, errors and discrepancies may not be completely excluded. If you come across any errors or discrepancies, please make a note of them and send them to our publishing office. We are constantly updating our manuscripts, eliminating errors, and improving quality.

Please contact us at the address above.

About the Cookbook Delights Series

The *Cookbook Delights Series* includes many different topics and themes. If you have a passion for food and wish to know more information about different foods, then this series of cookbooks will be beneficial to you. Each book features a different type of food, such as avocados, strawberries, huckleberries, salmon, vegetarian, lentils, almonds, cherries, coconuts, lemons, and many, many more.

The *Cookbook Delights Series* not only includes cookbooks about individual foods but also includes several holiday-themed cookbooks. Whatever your favorite holiday may be, chances are we have a cookbook with recipes designed with that holiday in mind. Some examples include *Halloween Delights, Thanksgiving Delights, Christmas Delights, Valentine Delights, Mother's Day Delights, St. Patrick's Day Delights,* and *Easter Delights.*

Each cookbook is designed for easy use and is organized into alphabetical sections. Over 250 recipes are included along with other interesting facts, folklore, and history of the featured food or theme. Each book comes with a beautiful full-color cover, ordering information, and a list of other upcoming books in the series.

Note cards, bookmarks, and a daily journal have been printed and are available to go along with each cookbook. You may view the entire line of cookbooks, journals, cards, posters, puzzles, and bookmarks by visiting our website at www.whisperingpinepress.com, or you can email us with your questions and your comments to: sales@whisperingpinepress.com.

Please ask your local bookstore to carry these sets of books.

To order, please contact:

Whispering Pine Press International, Inc.
c/o Valentine Delights: A Daily Journal
P.O. Box 214, Spokane Valley, WA 99037-0214
Phone: (509) 928-8700 | Fax: (509) 922-9949
Email: sales@WhisperingPinePress.com
Publisher Websites: www.WhisperingPinePress.com
www.WhisperingPinePressBookstore.com
Blog: www.WhisperingPinePressBlog.com
SAN 253-200X

We Invite You to Join the
Whispering Pine Press International, Inc.
Book Club!

Whispering Pine Press International, Inc.
c/o Valentine Delights: A Daily Journal
P.O. Box 214, Spokane Valley, WA 99037-0214
Phone: (509) 928-8700 | Fax: (509) 922-9949
Email: sales@WhisperingPinePress.com
Publisher Websites: www.WhisperingPinePress.com
www.WhisperingPinePressBookstore.com
Blog: www.WhisperingPinePressBlog.com

Buy 11 books and get the next one free, based on the average price of the first eleven purchased.

How the club works:

Simply use the order form below and order books from our catalog. You can buy just one at a time or all eleven at once. After the first eleven books are purchased, the next one is free. Please add shipping and handling as listed on this form. There are no purchase requirements at any time during your membership. Free book credit is based on the average price of the first eleven books purchased.

Join today! Pick your books and mail in the form today!

Yes! I want to join the Whispering Pine Press International, Inc., Book Club! Enroll me and send the books indicated below.

Title   Price

1. _____
2. _____
3. _____
4. _____
5. _____
6. _____
7. _____
8. _____
9. _____
10. _____
11. _____

Free Book Title: _____

Free Book Price: _____ Avg. Price: _____ Total Price: _____

Credit for the free book is based on the average price of the first 11 books purchased.

(Circle one) Check | Visa | MasterCard | Discover | American Express

Credit Card #: _____ Expiration Date: _____

Name: _____

Address: _____

City: _____ State: _____ Country: _____

Zip/Postal: _____ Phone: (_____) _____

Email: _____

Signature_____

Whispering Pine Press International, Inc.
Fundraising Opportunities

Fundraising cookbooks are proven moneymakers and great keepsake providers for your group. Whispering Pine Press International, Inc., offers a very special personalized cookbook fundraising program that encourages success to organizations all across the USA.

Our prices are competitive and fair. Currently, we offer a special of 100 books with many free features and excellent customer service. Any purchase you make is guaranteed first-rate.

Flexibility is not a problem. If you have special needs, we guarantee our cooperation in meeting each of them. Our goal is to create a cookbook that goes beyond your expectations. We have the confidence and a record that promises continual success.

Another great fundraising program is the *Cookbook Delights Series* Program. With cookbook orders of 50 copies or more, your organization receives a huge discount, making for a prompt and lucrative solution.

We also specialize in assisting group fundraising – Christian, community, nonprofit, and academic among them. If you are struggling for a new idea, something that will enhance your success and broaden your appeal, Whispering Pine Press International, Inc., can help.

For more information, write, phone, or fax to:

Whispering Pine Press International, Inc.
P.O. Box 214
Spokane Valley, WA 99037-0214
Phone: (509) 928-8700 | Fax: (509) 922-9949
Email: sales@WhisperingPinePress.com
Publisher Websites: www.WhisperingPinePress.com
www.WhisperingPinePressBookstore.com
Blog: www.WhisperingPinePressBlog.com
Book Website: www.ValentineDelights.com
SAN 253-200X

Personalized and/or Translated
Order Form for Any Book by
Whispering Pine Press International, Inc.

Dear Readers:

If you or your organization wishes to have this book or any other of our books personalized, we will gladly accommodate your needs. For instance, if you would like to change the names of the characters in a book to the names of the children in your family or Sunday school class, we would be happy to work with you on such a project. We can add more information of your choosing and customize this book especially for your family, group, or organization.

We are also offering an option of translating your book into another language. Please fill out the form below telling us exactly how you would like us to personalize your book.

Please send your request to:

Whispering Pine Press International, Inc.
c/o Valentine Delights: A Daily Journal
P.O. Box 214, Spokane Valley, WA 99037-0214
Phone: (509) 928-8700 | Fax: (509) 922-9949
Email: sales@WhisperingPinePress.com
Publisher Websites: www.WhisperingPinePress.com
www.WhisperingPinePressBookstore.com
Blog: www.WhisperingPinePressBlog.com

Person/Organization placing request: _____

_____Date: _____

Phone: (____) _____ Fax: (____)_____

Address: _____

City: _____ State: _____ Zip: _____

Language of the book: _____

Please explain your request in detail: _____

_____

_____

_____

CURRENT AND FUTURE BOOKS FOR ADULTS
by Karen Jean Matsko Hood

Hood Holiday Journal Series

Cookbook Delights Holiday Series

New Years Delights Journal – Book 1
Valentine Delights Journal – Book 2
St. Patrick's Day Delights Journal – Book 3
Easter Delights Journal – Book 4
Mother's Day Delights Journal - Book 5
Memorial Day Delights Journal – Book 6
Father's Day Delights Journal – Book 7
Fourth of July Delights Journal – Book 8
Labor Day Delights Journal – Book 9
Halloween Delights Journal – Book 10
Thanksgiving Delights Journal – Book 11
Christmas Delights Journal – Book 12

Hood Journal Series

Cookbook Delights Series

Apple Delights Journal – Book 1
Blueberry Delights – Book 2
Chocolate Delights Journal – Book 3
Coconut Delight Journal – Book 4
Grape Delights Journal – Book 5
Huckleberry Delights Journal – Book 6
Lentil Delights Journal – Book 7
Onion Delights Journal – Book 8
Peach Delights Journal – Book 9
Pear Delights Journal – Book 10
Plum Delights Journal – Book 11
Prickly Pear Delights Journal – Book 12
Pumpkin Delights Journal – Book 13
Raspberry Delights Journal – Book 14
Rhubarb Delights Journal – Book 15
Strawberry Delights Journal – Book 16
Tea Time Delights Journal – Book 17
Wine Delights Journal – Book 18
Winemaking Delights Journal – Book 19
Ethiopian Delights Journal – Book 20

Cookbooks

Cookbook Delights Series

Apple Delights – Book 1
Blueberry Delights – Book 2
Chocolate Delights – Book 3
Coconut Delights – Book 4
Grape Delights – Book 5
Huckleberry Delights – Book 6
Lentil Delights – Book 7
Onion Delights – Book 8
Peach Delights – Book 9
Pear Delights – Book 10
Plum Delights – Book 11
Prickly Pear Delights – Book 12
Pumpkin Delights – Book 13
Raspberry Delights – Book 14
Rhubarb Delights – Book 15
Strawberry Delights – Book 16
Tea Time Delights – Book 17
Wine Delights – Book 18
Winemaking Delights – Book 19
Ethiopian Delights – Book 20

Many of the above listed books are also available in bilingual and translated versions. Please contact Whispering Pine Press International, Inc., for details.

This list of books is not all-inclusive. For a complete list please visit our website or contact us at:

Whispering Pine Press International, Inc.
Your Northwest Book Publishing Company

P.O. Box 214, Spokane Valley, WA 99037-0214 USA
Phone: (509) 928-8700 | Fax: (509) 922-9949
Email: sales@whisperingpinepress.com

Publisher Websites
Main Website: WhisperingPinePress.com
Online Store: WhisperingPinePressBookstore.com
WordPress Blogs: WhisperingPinePressBlog.com
WhisperingPinePressKidsBooks.com
WhisperingPinePressTeenBooks.com
WhisperingPinePressPoetry.com

Author Websites
Karen Jean Matsko Hood
Author Website: KarenJeanMatskoHood.com
Online Store: KarenJeanMatskoHoodBookstore.com
Author Blog: KarenJeanMatskoHoodBlog.com
Kids Books: KarensKidsBooks.com
KarensTeensBooks.com

Author's Social Media
Friend her on **Facebook**: Karen Jean Matsko Hood Author Fan Page
Please Follow the Author on **Twitter**: @KarenJeanHood
Google Plus Profile: Karen Jean Matsko Hood

Pinterest.com/KarenJMHood

Valentine Delights
A Daily Journal
Hood Holiday Journal Series – Book 2

How to Order

Get your additional copies of this book by returning an order form and your check, money order, or credit card information to:

Whispering Pine Press International, Inc.
c/o Valentine Delights: A Daily Journal
P.O. Box 214, Spokane Valley, WA 99037-0214
Phone: (509) 928-8700 | Fax: (509) 922-9949
Email: sales@WhisperingPinePress.com
Publisher Websites: www.WhisperingPinePress.com
www.WhisperingPinePressBookstore.com
Blog: www.WhisperingPinePressBlog.com

Customer Name: _____

Address: _____

City, St., Zip: _____

Phone/Fax: _____

Email: _____

- -

Please send me _____ copies of _____ _____

_____ at $_____ per copy and $4.95 for shipping and handling per book, plus $2.95 each for additional books. Enclosed is my check, money order, or charge my account for $_____.

☐ Check   ☐ Money Order   ☐ Credit Card

(*Circle One*) MasterCard | Discover | Visa | American Express

☐☐☐☐   ☐☐☐☐   ☐☐☐☐   ☐☐☐☐

Expiration Date: _____

_____
Signature

_____
Print Name

Whispering Pine Press International, Inc. Order Form

Gift-wrapping, Autographing, and Inscription

We are proud to offer personal autographing by the author. For a limited time this service is absolutely free!
Gift-wrapping is also available for $4.95 per item.

1. Sold To

Name: _____
Street/Route: _____
_____
City: _____
State: _____ Zip: _____
Country: _____
Gift message: _____
_____
Email address: _____
Daytime Phone: (_ _) _ _ _-_ _ _ _
*Necessary for verifying orders
Home Phone: (_ _) _ _ _-_ _ _ _
Fax: (_ _) _ _ _-_ _ _ _

2. Ship To

☐ Is this a new or corrected address?

☐ Alternative Shipping Address

☐ Mailing Address

Name: _____
Address: _____
_____
City: _____
State: _____ Zip: _____
Country: _____
Email address: _____

3. Items Ordered

ISBN # /Item #	Size	Color	Qty.	Title or Description	Price	Total

4. Method Of Payment

International, Inc. (No Cash or COD's)

☐ Visa ☐ MasterCard ☐ Discover ☐ American Express ☐ Check/Money Order

Please make it payable to Whispering Pine Press International, Inc. (No Cash or COD's)

Account Number   Expiration Date

_____ / _____
Month Year

☐☐☐☐☐ ☐☐☐☐☐ ☐☐☐☐☐ ☐☐☐☐

Signature_____
Cardholder's signature

Printed Name_____
Please print name of cardholder

Address of Cardholder_____

Subtotal	
Gift wrap $4.95 Each	
For delivery in WA add 8.7% sales tax.	
Shipping See chart at left	
6. Total	

5. Shipping & Handling

Continental US

US Postal Ground: For books please add $4.95 for the first book and $2.95 each for additional books.
All non-book items, add 15% of the Subtotal.
Please allow 1-4 weeks for delivery.
US Postal Air: Please add $15.00 shipping and handling.
Please allow 1-3 days for delivery.
Alaska, Hawaii, and the US Territories By Ship:
Please add 10% shipping and handling
(minimum charge $15.00).

Please
By Air: Please add 12% shipping and handling (minimum charge $15.00).
Please allow 2 –6 weeks for delivery.
International By Ship: Please add 10% shipping and handling (minimum charge $15.00).
Please allow 6-12 weeks for delivery.
By Air: Please add 12% shipping and handling (minimum charge $15.00).
Please allow 2-6 weeks for delivery.
FedEx Shipments: Add $5.00 to the above airmail charges for overnight delivery.

Shop Online:
www.whisperingpinepress.com
Fax orders to: (509) 922-9949

Whispering Pine Press International, Inc.
P.O. Box 214
Spokane Valley, WA 99037-0214 USA
Phone: (509) 928-8700 • Fax: (509) 922-9949
Email: sales@whisperingpinepress.com
Website: www.whisperingpinepress.com

About the Author and Cook

Karen Jean Matsko Hood has always enjoyed cooking, baking, and experimenting with recipes. At this time Hood is working to complete a series of cookbooks that blends her skills and experience in cooking and entertaining. Hood entertains large groups of people and especially enjoys designing creative menus with holiday, international, ethnic, and regional themes.

Hood is publishing a cookbook series entitled the *Cookbook Delights Series*, in which each cookbook emphasizes a different food ingredient or theme. The first cookbook in the series is *Apple Delights Cookbook*. Hood is working to complete another series of cookbooks titled *Hood and Matsko Family Cookbooks*, which includes many recipes handed down from her family heritage and others that have emerged from more current family traditions. She has been invited to speak on talk radio shows on various topics, and favorite recipes from her cookbooks have been prepared on local television programs.

Hood was born and raised in Great Falls, Montana. As an undergraduate, she attended the College of St. Benedict in St. Joseph, Minnesota, and St. John's University in Collegeville, Minnesota. She attended the University of Great Falls in Great Falls, Montana. Hood received a B.S. Degree in Natural Science from the College of St. Benedict and minored in both Psychology and Secondary Education. Upon her graduation, Hood and her husband taught science and math on the island of St. Croix in the U.S. Virgin Islands. Hood has completed postgraduate classes at the University of Iowa in Iowa City, Iowa. In May 2001, she completed her Master's Degree in Pastoral Ministry at Gonzaga University in Spokane, Washington. She has taken postgraduate classes at Lewis and Clark College on the North Idaho college campus in Coeur d'Alene, Idaho, Taylor University in Fort Wayne, Indiana, Spokane Falls Community College, Spokane Community College, Washington State University, University of Washington, and Eastern Washington University. Hood is working on research projects to complete her Ph.D. in Leadership Studies at Gonzaga University in Spokane, Washington.

Hood resides in Greenacres, Washington, along with her husband, many of her sixteen children, and foster children. Her interests include writing, research, and teaching. She previously has volunteered as a court advocate in the Spokane juvenile court system for abused and neglected children. Hood is a literary advocate for youth and adults. Her hobbies include cooking, baking, collecting, photography, indoor and outdoor gardening, farming, and the cultivation of unusual flowering plants and orchids. She enjoys raising several specialty breeds of animals including Babydoll Southdown, Friesen, and Icelandic sheep, Icelandic horses, bichons frisés, cockapoos, Icelandic sheepdogs, a Newfoundland, a Rottweiler, a variety of Nubian and fainting goats, and a few rescue cats. Hood also enjoys bird-watching and finds all aspects of nature precious.

She demonstrates a passionate appreciation of the environment and a respect for all life. She also invites you to visit her websites:

www.KarenJeanMatskoHood.com

www.KarenJeanMatskoHoodBookstore.com

www.KarenJeanMatskoHoodBlog.com

www.facebook.com/KarenJeanMatskoHoodAuthorFanPage

www.KarensKidsBooks.com

www.HoodFamilyBlog.com

www.HoodFamily.com

Author's Social Media

Friend her on **Facebook**: Karen Jean Matsko Hood Author Fan Page

Please Follow the Author on **Twitter**: @KarenJeanHood

Google Plus Profile: Karen Jean Matsko Hood

Pinterest.com/KarenJMHood

www.ingramcontent.com/pod-product-compliance
Lightning Source LLC
LaVergne TN
LVHW051643080426
835511LV00016B/2463